# TEENS
# SHARE
# THE WORD

# TEENS
# SHARE
# THE WORD

Compiled and edited by
Maria Grace Dateno, FSP
and Emily Marsh

Pauline
BOOKS & MEDIA
Boston

Library of Congress Cataloging-in-Publication Data

Teens share the Word / compiled and edited by Maria Grace Dateno and
Emily Marsh.

p. cm.

ISBN 0-8198-7437-X (pbk.)

1. Bible--Meditations. 2. Catholic teenagers--Prayers and devotions.
I. Dateno, Maria Grace. II. Marsh, Emily.

BS491.5.T34 2011

242'.63--dc22

2010038175

Unless otherwise noted, the Scripture quotations contained herein are from the
*New Revised Standard Version Bible: Catholic Edition*, copyright © 1989, 1993,
Division of Christian Education of the National Council of the Churches of Christ
in the United States of America. Used by permission. All rights reserved.

Scripture quotations noted as NAB are taken from the *New American Bible with
Revised New Testament and Revised Psalms* © 1991, 1986, 1970, Confraternity of
Christian Doctrine, Washington, D.C., and are used by permission of the copyright
owner. All rights reserved. No part of the *New American Bible* may be reproduced
in any form without permission in writing from the copyright owner.

Cover design by Rosana Usselmann

Cover photo by Robyn Mackenzie/istockphoto.com

Published by Pauline Books & Media, 50 Saint Pauls Avenue, Boston, MA 02130-
3491. www.pauline.org

Printed in the U.S.A.

Pauline Books & Media is the publishing house of the Daughters of St. Paul, an
international congregation of women religious serving the Church with the
communications media.

1 2 3 4 5 6 7 8 9                                              15 14 13 12 11

# CONTENTS

# INTRODUCTION

## How can we know God?

One of the most important ways God has revealed himself to us is through Sacred Scripture, also known as the Bible. We call Scripture the Word of God because it is not like any other book ever written. It's actually a collection of books written over a period of many centuries. The human beings who wrote the Bible were the ones who put the words down on paper (or whatever they used to write on back then!), but it is God who speaks to us through them, using the gifts and minds and writing of the human authors to reveal himself. That's what we mean when we say the Bible is inspired. And that's why the Bible inspires us when we read it today.

The Word of God can touch us like no other book can. And once we have been touched by it, we cannot keep to ourselves how it has changed us. We want to testify to the power and love we have experienced.

The teens who contributed to this book all have experienced the power of the Word of God in their lives, and now they share it with you.

# GOD'S LOVE
# AND PRESENCE

# A PRAYER OF GODS LOVE

. . . that Christ may dwell in your hearts
   through faith,
as you are being rooted and grounded in love.
I pray that you may have the power to
   comprehend,
      with all the saints,
what is the breadth and length and height
   and depth,
and to know the love of Christ that surpasses
   knowledge,
so that you may be filled with all the fullness
   of God.
Now to him who by the power at work within us
is able to accomplish abundantly far more
than all we can ask or imagine,
to him be glory in the church
and in Christ Jesus to all generations,
forever and ever. Amen.

*Ephesians 3:17–21*

# God knows me and loves me

*"O LORD, you have searched me and known me. You know when I sit down and when I rise up; you discern my thoughts from far away. . . . Even before a word is on my tongue, O LORD, you know it completely"* (Psalm 139:1–2, 4).

The fact that God knows every little thing about me never ceases to amaze me. He knows me better than I know myself. There are so many times in my life when I have to try to figure out how to deal with a difficult situation, but remembering that God has searched every little part of me and understands my thoughts even when I don't puts me at ease, because I know he has everything under control. These words free me from trying to hide myself and be somebody that I am not. God loves everything about me and wants me to be as happy as possible.

~ *Elyse*

## God lives within me

*"Can it indeed be that God dwells among men on earth? If the heavens and the highest heavens cannot contain you, how much less this temple which I have built!" (1 Kings 8:27 NAB).*

This verse, which Solomon prayed to God in the presence of the people of Israel at the dedication of the Temple, serves as a beautiful reflection for Holy Communion. Here Solomon speaks of the Temple he built; we are temples of the Holy Spirit. When we receive Holy Communion, God, whom the entire universe cannot contain, comes to dwell inside our bodies. This meditation gives me a greater feeling of awe and gratefulness to God for deigning to make his abode in the humble temple of my soul.

～ *Kimberly*

## Jesus is always with us

*"For where your treasure is, there your heart will be also"* *(Matthew 6:21).*

This quote touches me because I think it is very true. Many people seek materialistic things. Some people want more and more and yet are never satisfied. What they do not realize is that none of those things is truly what the heart desires. Our treasure and source of true happiness is heaven with Jesus. Thinking deeper into the meaning of the quote, I realize that our essential treasure is Jesus and that Jesus is always present in our hearts. So we are seeking for no reason at all, because what we've been seeking has always been with us, in our hearts.

~ *Cristina*

## God's love is generous

*"Is there anyone among you who, if your child asks for a fish, will give a snake instead of a fish? Or if the child asks for an egg, will give a scorpion? If you then, who are evil, know how to give good gifts to your children, how much more will the heavenly Father give the Holy Spirit to those who ask him!" (Luke 11:11–13).*

This verse deals with God's being ever present and willing to help us whenever we ask for it. It really touches me personally because of how it seems to suggest in strong terms just how awesome God's presence in my life can be. It leaves this presence a mystery but firmly reassures me of God's fatherly care and promises even more. It is a humbling verse that provides a strong metaphor for God's love, making it very simple for me to relate to.

~ *Colin*

# God is on your side

*"The LORD, your God, is in your midst, a warrior who gives victory; he will rejoice over you with gladness, he will renew you in his love . . ." (Zephaniah 3:17).*

This Scripture passage speaks to me. I think that if we modernized this it would pretty much mean that God is always with you. He will be joyful about your presence and fill in any love that has been lost. It speaks to me because this really is proof that God is on your side, so even when you're in a tough time and it seems like there's no way out, God will find a way to fix it.

∼ *Danielle*

## Jesus calls me his friend!

*"No one has greater love than this, to lay down one's life for one's friends. You are my friends if you do what I command you. . . . I have called you friends, because I have made known to you everything that I have heard from my Father" (John 15:13–15).*

This is so beautiful to me, that Jesus would call me his friend. Jesus, in all of his power and glory, called lowly me, a sinner, his friend. He didn't say that I'm an acquaintance, or just another person his Father made, or just some other kid he had to lay down his life for. Jesus said that *I'm his friend*—someone he loves and knows personally, and desires a relationship with. To me, this is an overwhelming statement, especially when friends let me down or hurt me, to know that I always have a best Friend who is constantly with me, loving me perfectly, never failing me, and always understanding everything I am, even my weak-nesses and fears. He is always just waiting for me to acknowledge his love and presence. He did the greatest thing anyone's ever done for me: saved my life by giving up his.

∼ *Mia*

# God is there for us when no one else is

*"The rain fell, the floods came, and the winds blew and beat on that house, but it did not fall, because it had been founded on rock"* (Matthew 7:25).

If we live our lives for God completely, then our lives are like a house built on a rock. No matter how tough or hard times may get, we will still stand firm in God's arms. I remember a time when I felt abandoned, and the only one I felt was really there for me was God.

~ *Miguel*

# When someone you love dies

*"In my Father's house there are many dwelling places. If it were not so, would I have told you that I go to prepare a place for you? And if I go and prepare a place for you, I will come again and will take you to myself, so that where I am, there you may be also"* (John 14:2–3).

My older brother died in a car accident two years ago. This passage in the Bible is what helped me get through that time and still helps me now. It's Jesus talking to his disciples before he died. They didn't know what was going to happen, but I'm sure it helped them afterward to remember that Jesus had said this. Sometimes it helps me to imagine my brother saying that last part to me: "so that where I am, there you may be also." When I really miss him, I imagine the two of us together again in heaven, in the place Jesus has prepared for us, happy forever.

$\sim$ *Kevin*

## God loves me even when I make mistakes

*"She said, 'May I prove worthy of your kindness, my lord: you have comforted me, your servant, with your consoling words; would indeed that I were a servant of yours!'"* (Ruth 2:13 NAB).

There are so many situations in my life when even my best doesn't seem enough. Whether it's a test I studied hard for and didn't do well on, or a math problem I failed to explain correctly to my sister, I can name so many times when even my best just doesn't seem to cut it. It's difficult to recognize that even during these times, God is still proud of my efforts.

Even when I'm not pleased with the outcomes of my own performances, Ruth reminds me in this passage that God is pleased because he knows that no human, including me, is perfect. Knowing this is comforting. God will not leave me alone and will not abandon me. In this passage, Ruth is so thankful to Boaz for recognizing her small contribution and responding to it with kindness. Even though Ruth was afraid that her best wasn't enough, God worked through Boaz to reward her and comfort her, reminding her that he was still proud of her. In the same way, even when my efforts seem hopeless, I need to remember God is watching what I do, and he applauds my attempts to live his Word.

~ *Lauren*

## God comforts us in times of trouble

*"I have said this to you, so that in me you may have peace. In the world you face persecution. But take courage; I have conquered the world!" (John 16:33).*

This Scripture verse has had a very large impact on me for multiple reasons. The first reason is because I can relate to it so easily, because I know that I will have trouble throughout my lifetime, but if I just believe in the Lord and his plan for me, then I can have courage and strength in him. The second reason is because a very powerful experience that I had at my youth group was based on this Scripture. Youth group has changed my life. I was at rock bottom during the middle of my sophomore year; then I started going to my youth group, and I have been changed so much. Through my youth group I have made my best friends in the entire world, gone on a mission trip to Nicaragua, and foremost made a deep spiritual connection with my Lord. This Scripture passage really speaks to me also because I have had so many struggles in my life, and before I found God I did not know where to turn. After God so graciously took me into his loving arms, I realized that I can turn to him in any situation and time of need and I will find comfort . . . maybe not immediately, but eventually I will, because God works in mysterious ways. I turn to this verse whenever I feel down and think that there is no one I can turn to. When I read this I remember that God is always going to be there for me because of his endless mercy and love. There is nothing better than that.

~ *Brigid*

# God gives us the love we desire

*"Whoever does not love does not know God, for God is love" (1 John 4:8).*

What is written in this verse is all that God calls us to do in life. To simply love. Mother Teresa once said that the poorest of the poor is the man who does not know Jesus, and that the greatest poverty is the feeling of being unloved. When you think about it, there are many people suffering from material poverty all over the world. And yet, every single one of us comes to suffer from emotional and spiritual poverty at certain points of our lives. There are times when we feel empty and unwanted. Our hearts search for comfort, and we seek consolation. Sometimes we turn to the wrong people, or end up turning to the wrong things. Yet, we finally come to realize it is love that we desire. We all want to be loved. So many people in the world are broken and crushed because they lack love, because they lack God in their lives. What they lack is true love, and it is only God who possesses true love, for "God is love." So the next time we go searching for love, let's search for God.

&#8767; *Cherubim*

# GUIDANCE

# A PRAYER FOR GUIDANCE

Blessed be the God and Father
of our Lord Jesus Christ,
who . . . chose us in Christ
before the foundation of the world
to be holy and blameless before him in love.
With all wisdom and insight he has made known
    to us
the mystery of his will,
according to his good pleasure that he set forth
    in Christ,
as a plan for the fullness of time,
to gather up all things in him,
things in heaven and things on earth.

*Ephesians 1:3–4, 8–10*

## God's strength upholds us

*"He gives power to the faint, and strengthens the powerless. Even youths will faint and be weary, and the young will fall exhausted; but those who wait for the* Lord *shall renew their strength, they shall mount up with wings like eagles, they shall run and not be weary, they shall walk and not faint" (Isaiah 40:29–31).*

When most people hear the word "strength," they think of an athlete, someone with overwhelming physical ability. The fact of the matter is there is no athlete in the world who would have success on or off the field without Jesus Christ. That is what this passage says to me. I may not be the most talented player on the field, but I know for certain that when I put a concern in his hands, Jesus will give me the moral and spiritual strength that I need to complete my task.

*∼ Joe*

## God is always leading us

*"Those whose steps are guided by the Lord; whose way God approves, may stumble, but they will never fall, for the Lord holds their hand" (Psalm 37:23–24 NAB).*

My two elder siblings left for college this year, one to a different country and one for the first time. I am very close to my siblings, so, having a hard time coping, I spent every night the week before they left searching God's Sacred Scripture for something to encourage them, and comfort me. Finally God led me to this verse. Reading it, I was reminded that God was leading my sister and brother, and no matter what, he is going to hold their hands. They are on the paths God has chosen for them, the paths they need to follow. If that means they must leave me for a while, so be it. I knew they were going to places where they would have many hands to hold them up.

On the other hand, my brother and sister are my greatest role models, and I was afraid that by losing them, I might fall away from God's path for me. The second part of this verse helped me combat that fear. All of us may stumble this year, but we will never fall. My littlest brother is twenty months old and still needs help walking down stairs and such. We hold his hand to make sure that if he trips, he does not hurt himself. God does the same for us. He holds all of our hands. Now this verse has become a theme song for me, and it is a reminder of the love of my siblings as well as the love of my God.

~ *Olivia*

## God speaks hope to us

*"Jesus said to her, 'I am the resurrection and the life. Those who believe in me, even though they die, will live, and everyone who lives and believes in me will never die'"* (John 11:25–26).

I believe this passage because I was going through a rough time in my life when going to church was more of a physical action than a spiritual one. I was sitting in church one Sunday and the priest was giving his homily. While I was gazing off into space, the words "I am the resurrection and the life. Those who believe in me, even though they die, will live" stuck out to me. It was as if God was trying to give me a message of hope which would bring me happiness and peace. He was telling me that if I live and believe in Christ then my spirit will never die, and I will always find comfort and happiness in God because he grants eternal life to those who believe in him.

~ *Jason*

# God opens doors for us

*"For nothing will be impossible with God" (Luke 1:37).*

This Scripture verse speaks to me in a special way. Our family's dream has always been to adopt a baby born with Down syndrome. We knew that if this was God's will, he could somehow make this happen. My parents simply submitted our home study for consideration, and then we prayed and waited. Ten months later, God opened the door for us, and the adoption was finalized last summer. Our family now includes a happy baby boy with that special extra chromosome, to remind us that nothing, absolutely nothing, is impossible with God.

~ *Richard*

# My future is in God's hands

*"For surely I know the plans I have for you, says the LORD, plans for your welfare and not for harm, to give you a future with hope"* (Jeremiah 29:11).

These words serve as a great beacon of hope to me, as they seem to be speaking directly to my heart. As a junior in high school I am being faced with making many difficult decisions—college, choosing a major, stay home, leave home—and with all these choices it's no surprise how overwhelming it can be.

Knowing that each path I choose to walk will inevitably shape and determine my future is a very frightening thought. So often I procrastinate doing this very thing out of fear of the outcome. This passage from Jeremiah reminds me that my future lies solely in God's hands and that as long as I believe, trust, and obey him, he will take my hand and lead me to where I'm supposed to be.

*～ Rebekah*

# Making media choices

*"Do not be conformed to this world, but be transformed by the renewing of your minds, so that you may discern what is the will of God—what is good and acceptable and perfect" (Romans 12:2).*

I don't know about you, but I don't want to conform—to do what everyone else is doing. I want to do the will of God so that I can help transform the world. One place it's hard for me not to conform is in the movies I watch. I know I should think about how it will affect my mind—whether it's "good and acceptable," not just if it's what everyone else is going to see. How can we transform the world if we're just going along with everyone else?

So, I ask God, is this good for me? Will this transform my mind in a good way, or will I be stuck with images and ideas that aren't good swimming around my head? And hopefully I have the strength to do the right thing, and not just what the world expects.

∼ *Katie*

# God guides me through others

*"[Andrew] brought Simon to Jesus . . ." (John 1:42).*

When I think about it, there are a lot of people in my life who have brought me to Jesus: my parents, who had me baptized; the religion teacher who prepared me for First Communion; my grandfather, who acted as my sponsor for Confirmation a couple of years ago; my best friend, who is a major source of encouragement for me in my faith. But most recently, I have realized how Jesus guides me through people in my daily life. When I want to sleep in on a Sunday morning, and my parents wake me up to go to church, that is God guiding me. Or when I want to play video games instead of studying for a test, but my friend offers to study with me, that is God guiding me. Or even when I am feeling down, and my friend stops by or calls or texts just to see how I'm doing, he is guiding me closer to God by being an example of love and concern. I may not always see this as being brought to

Jesus, and I may not always even like it, but it really is guidance from God. I think that the important thing is to try to recognize how Jesus is guiding me, so that I can bring people to Jesus, too.

∽ *Chris*

## Be God's voice for others

*"When they hand you over, do not worry about how you are to speak or what you are to say; for what you are to say will be given to you at that time" (Matthew 10:19).*

This Bible verse is just as applicable today, even though we might not be preaching in front of crowds or facing persecution. This particular verse has helped me when I am about to give presentations or speak in front of people, but also for something much more important than that. When friends come to us with their problems, how do we help them? When we know others are struggling with something, what do we say to them? How do we know how to help someone when they won't tell us anything? How do we establish trust with someone who doubts that we actually want to help them? How can we be God's voice for others? This Bible verse assures us: Jesus will tell us what to say. Listen thoughtfully to others, and then to

God. What does he want to say to that person? He will make it known to us. Then, when we say it, God will speak through us. It will touch our heart and that of the other person. It will build God's family. I have experienced it—it is true. We will become the ears and voice of God, if we take the time to listen.

∼ *Fara*

## God has plans for me

*"It is too light a thing that you should be my servant to raise up the tribes of Jacob and to restore the survivors of Israel; I will give you as a light to the nations, that my salvation may reach to the end of the earth"* (Isaiah 49:6).

This is one of my favorite Scripture passages. It is an inspiring verse by itself, but it is especially significant to me as a young person discerning my vocation. I am sixteen years old and starting to think seriously about the future. So many possibilities beckon to me. In the midst of them, I am struggling to discover God's will and to find the courage to obey him. In all of my uncertainty and trepidation, these words, written under the inspiration of the Holy Spirit centuries ago, speak to me today. God has a plan for me. He wants to make me "a light to the nations." He desires to give to me a part to play in helping his salvation "reach to the end of the earth." He will give me the courage and the wisdom necessary to do his will. I was created for a purpose, and not only will God reveal my purpose to me, but he will also empower me to fulfill it.

～ James

# TRUST

# A PRAYER OF TRUST

The LORD is my light and my salvation;
    whom shall I fear?
The LORD is the stronghold of my life;
    of whom shall I be afraid?
When evildoers assail me
    to devour my flesh—
my adversaries and foes—
    they shall stumble and fall.
Though an army encamp against me,
    my heart shall not fear;
though war rise up against me,
    yet I will be confident.
One thing I asked of the LORD,
    that will I seek after:
to live in the house of the LORD
    all the days of my life,
to behold the beauty of the LORD,
    and to inquire in his temple.

*Psalm 27:1–4*

## Live the present moment

*"Therefore, do not be anxious about tomorrow, for tomorrow will be anxious for itself. Let the day's own trouble be sufficient for the day"* (Matthew 6:34 RSV).

It's seventh period, school's almost over, and every student is anxious for the last bell to ring . . . wouldn't you be, too? God doesn't want us to be anxious, because he wants us to live our lives in the present moment. When you live your life waiting for some other day to come, you miss what happens in the present. Live the life God wants you to live and wait to see what he has in store for you.

~ *Stephanie*

## Put your worries in God's hands

*"Do not worry about anything, but in everything by prayer and supplication with thanksgiving let your requests be made known to God. And the peace of God, which surpasses all understanding, will guard your hearts and your minds in Christ Jesus" (Philippians 4:6–7).*

I constantly find myself worrying about everything. I worry about academics and athletics. I am overloaded with homework and practices. I stress over pleasing my parents, teachers, coaches, and friends. I worry about pleasing everyone and trying to be perfect. On top of that, what am I supposed to do with my life and where am I supposed to go to college?

In the midst of all this worry, I tell myself that prayer is just another thing I have to do or another thing I have to worry about. But this Scripture verse always runs through my head. These words remind me that prayer is the most important thing in my life, not only because it is communication with my Father, but because my worries are put in his hands. Knowing that God is taking care of everything for me, I am free to live, and my heart and mind are guarded in Christ Jesus.

∼ *Allisyn*

## We don't have to be afraid

*"I hereby command you: Be strong and courageous; do not be frightened or dismayed, for the LORD your God is with you wherever you go"* (Joshua 1:9).

God has a plan for all of us and at times his plans can seem scary. I constantly find myself feeling fear and hopelessness when God brings forth a challenge in my life, but by his grace, I found this verse a couple of years ago when I was trying to read a little bit of the Bible each day to help me in my spiritual life. The words really touched me, and they have helped me so much whenever I have felt alone in my struggles. This verse tells us that we are never alone and that we never have to be afraid. God has a path for all of us. He will never present us with an obstacle that is greater than our own strengths, and he is with us every step of the way. Whether it's a test at school, dealing with family problems, or even God calling us to the seemingly impossible, we don't have to be afraid. We know that the Creator of the universe is on our side.

∼ *Hannah*

# Nothing is too big for God

*"I have told you this so that you might have peace in me. In the world you will have trouble, but take courage, I have conquered the world"* (John 16:33 NAB).

Sometimes, it seems like my world is crashing down around me and there isn't any way that I can go on. In times like these, I turn to Jesus and hand everything over to him. It's not always easy to relinquish control, and often I try to handle the situation myself. But this world, which often seems so difficult and painful to me, poses no challenge for my Lord, who has already overcome any obstacle that I may face. Nothing is too big for my God. His love for me is so great that he follows me around with his arms outstretched, and I take comfort in knowing that every time I stumble and fall, Jesus is there to pick me up. I have complete peace in Jesus, knowing that no matter what I do, he is there to love and support me.

$\sim$ *Amanda*

# I can depend on God forever

*"For you, O LORD, are my hope, my trust, O LORD, from my youth" (Psalm 71:5).*

When I read these words, I know that they are true. They help me to know that I can trust and believe in God always. When I feel sad or scared I can turn to this verse and know that I can trust in God.

The trust I have in God is different from the trust I have in other people, like my family or friends. The trust I have in family and friends I'm not always sure I can depend on forever. Maybe for a little while, but the trust I have in God lasts . . . forever.

When you know that you have Someone looking out for you, it makes you feel good. But it's not just you he's looking out for. God watches over everybody.

$\sim$ *Shamiah*

## God provides—trust in him

*"But strive first for the kingdom of God and his right-eousness, and all these things will be given to you as well" (Matthew 6:33).*

In these difficult economic times, many people suffer anxiety over what will become of their homes, jobs, and their future. My own family is going through tough financial times, so this is something I know well. However, God never abandons those who put their trust in him, and he always provides. This I also know since I have witnessed in my own family how, even through serious difficulties, we have never lacked the essentials. God wants us to spend more time seeking him and his kingdom, living his gifts to the fullest, and spreading love, compassion, and mercy to others, especially now. Worrying is easy; trusting God with our basic needs can be tough. However, worrying doesn't get us anything; it doesn't solve our problems. I pray that God will always let me rest my life, and my family's, in his loving hands. I ask the Lord to give me peace in the turbulent times, and to help me trust him and have the conviction that he will never allow us to suffer for lack of the basic needs.

Lord, be with me, protect me and my family, provide all that we need to survive, and above all, protect our hearts and souls from anxiety. We trust in you!

∾ *Gabriel*

## We can do all things with God

*"Listen to the sound of my cry, my King and my God, for to you I pray"* (Psalm 5:2).

When I read this verse, I know that God is always there and is always listening. In my life I have encountered some tough bumps, and even though sometimes things were bad, I knew God was right there with me, saying, "You can do it, because I am right here!" No matter what the situation is now, or what situation is coming, if you believe and trust he is with you, everything will be okay! You will be able to succeed in everything with him!

~ Ashleigh

# Faith in God overcomes everything

*"Do not let your hearts be troubled. You have faith in God; have faith also in me" (John 14:1 NAB).*

This short, inspiring Bible verse has always been a key idea in my life. Whenever I have a problem, I think of this short saying. In these few words, Jesus speaks to me and shows me there is nothing to be afraid of. My faith in God can conquer all the problems I face. It also reminds me that God is my strength. There is nothing I cannot do if I have God by my side.

*∼ Dominic*

## We have every reason to trust God

*"Look at the birds of the air; they neither sow nor reap nor gather into barns, and yet your heavenly Father feeds them. Are you not of more value than they?"* (Matthew 6:26).

This is absolutely true! If you really think about it, birds are a perfect example of trust. They do not worry about what they will eat the next day or how much money they have. In the winter, some fly south while others are equipped to survive the winter. They simply live one day at a time and are content.

I think that we should be like the "birds of the air," always trusting that God will take care of us no matter what. He promised to be with us always. If God provides for the birds, how much more will he provide for humans, who are made in his image and likeness? The last time I went to Adoration, I was stressed about school. But I soon felt a sense of surrender and peace. I knew that God had everything under control. We have every reason to trust in God because he said he would provide for us.

*∾ Olivia*

## God will never turn me away

*"Cast all your anxiety on him, because he cares for you"* (1 Peter 5:7).

Reading this powerful passage makes me really think about how much God truly cares for me. It reveals to me exactly how much I can trust in him. I can put my whole life in his hands. I can pour out my heart, my soul, my wildest and most laughable dreams, and he won't laugh at me. I can seek refuge in him, and he will not turn me away. God comforts me in my sadness and aids me in my difficulties. In him I become whole because he cares for me.

~ *Angela*

# The hope of heaven

*" . . . no eye has seen, nor ear heard, nor the human heart conceived, what God has prepared for those who love him" (1 Corinthians 2:9).*

When I feel really bummed or overwhelmed with life, this verse reminds me that heaven is what I have to look forward to. Take a minute to imagine what you think heaven will be like. God has made this wonderful "place" for us to be with him forever. This verse says that we can't even conceive of how great it will be. In heaven there will be no sorrow or fear, only joy, happiness, and peace. God will answer all our questions. Remembering this gives me hope to continue on to my future. I remind myself that no problem lasts forever, and the reward of being faithful will totally be worth it.

$\sim$ *Marcus*

## Jesus can get me through anything

*"I can do all things through him who strengthens me"*
*(Philippians 4:13).*

This Bible verse is very important in my life. These words inspire me, strengthen me, and help me persevere in many different times in my life. Whenever I feel like I cannot go on, or that things are pointless, or any other discouraging thought enters my head, I think of these words, and they brighten up my life. These words teach me that Christ is always with me, and that he will get me through anything. Alone, I am nothing, but with Christ, I can do anything.

$\sim$ *Natalie*

# TEMPTATION

# A PRAYER IN TIMES OF TEMPTATION

Therefore, to keep me from being too elated,
a thorn was given me in the flesh,
a messenger of Satan to torment me,
to keep me from being too elated.
Three times I appealed to the Lord about this,
that it would leave me, but he said to me,
"My grace is sufficient for you,
for power is made perfect in weakness."
So, I will boast all the more gladly of my
    weaknesses,
so that the power of Christ may dwell in me.
Therefore I am content with weaknesses, insults,
    hardships,
persecutions, and calamities for the sake of
    Christ;
for whenever I am weak, then I am strong.

*2 Corinthians 12:7–10*

# Stand firm in your faith

*"If you do not stand firm in faith, you shall not stand at all" (Isaiah 7:9).*

This verse from Isaiah got me through a rough patch in my life. I was having a hard time getting myself to go to church. I thought maybe I could just take a break from it. But, for some reason, I just kept going. That is when I found this verse and realized that God does want me at church. Just because you don't feel the relationship with God growing doesn't mean you should give up. After all, what do you have, if not your faith?

⌒ *Meghan*

## Am I living like Jesus?

*"He stretched out his hand and touched him, saying, 'I do choose. Be made clean!' Immediately his leprosy was cleansed"* (Matthew 8:3).

The two major questions this story raises are "Do I reach out and show God's love to others?" and "Do I stand up for my faith even if it's not the popular thing to do?"

My answer to the second question is absolutely yes. I don't care what people think about me or my faith. I almost always stand up for God, and if I don't, it's due to internal spiritual conflicts—not peer pressure.

My answer to the first question is not as good, however. I don't always treat people the way I'd want to be treated, and this is something I need to work on. Sometimes I can be judgmental and treat others based on their appearance or social status. Jesus wouldn't have done this. He hung out with lepers, prostitutes, and people of other religions. He shared God's love with everyone even if it made others think poorly of him. I need to be like this. It's wrong to hold back my kindness and love for others because someone is different or unpopular. I promise to work on this. Scripture is just overflowing with life lessons.

*∾ Lisa*

## Peer pressure

*"For freedom Christ has set us free" (Galatians 5:1).*

There's a lot of pressure in today's society to be "cool" or popular: you have to wear the right clothes, hang out with the right people, be involved in the right activities. Sometimes popularity even means engaging in dangerous behavior (like drinking or doing drugs), or being unkind and treating certain types of people like outcasts. With so much pressure coming from every corner of society, how am I supposed to live my life in freedom? But that's what this verse from Galatians is talking about when it says "Christ has set us free."

Christ did not come to earth and suffer and die and rise so that we could be pressured into doing dangerous or sinful things. He came to give us the ultimate freedom! I have to ask myself why I do what I do—if I do it because it's pleasing to God, or because it's going to make me popular. Then, when I feel like I don't have the strength to resist all the pressure to be popular, I can remember that Christ has already set me free.

∼ *Caleb*

## Put God first

*"Do not store up for yourselves treasures on earth, where moth and rust consume and where thieves break in and steal" (Matthew 6:19).*

This quote tells the complete truth. We must all remember not to treasure our material things so much because we can lose them in an instant. However, our spiritual goods should be treasured the most because we can't lose this treasure. The more I thought about this quote the more I realized how true it is that people spend most of their time on earth worrying about buying the next new thing. You always hear people say, I want a new phone, I want a new car, but you rarely hear, I want to spend the rest of the day with God in prayer or I want to go to Mass so that I can spend time with God. You can always lose or break your phone or car. However, you'll never lose that time you spent with God in prayer. We should all try to start treasuring spiritual things instead of material things. It's something hard to do, but we must always remember that with God in our lives, anything is possible.

〜 *Miguelangel*

## Jesus calls us out of sin

*"Young man, I say to you, rise!" (Luke 7:14).*

This quote has a great message. To me this is Jesus speaking to us young people, encouraging us to rise up to glory and away from evil and sin. As teenagers we encounter a lot of temptation and sin. If we fall down into sin, Jesus will always give us another chance to come back to him. Even when we think we can't see the light of God, Jesus will tell us to rise, and we can.

*∼ Shawna*

# My body is a gift from God

*"... glorify God in your body" (1 Corinthians 6:20).*

A priest once gave me this idea, and I've been doing it ever since: Every time I make the Sign of the Cross, I think of this quote from the Bible— "glorify God in your body." It's a good reminder for me, especially in a moment of temptation. I belong to God. My body is a gift from God, and I want everything I do with it to give honor and glory to God, and not be something that hurts other people or myself, or something that I'm ashamed of afterward.

∼ *Brendan*

## I am a temple of the Holy Spirit

*"For God's temple is holy, and you are that temple"*
*(1 Corinthians 3:17).*

The media tell us the exact opposite of this
verse. The media sends the message that our bodies
are supposed to be strong and muscular, gorgeous
and sexy, and basically perfect. From the media,
we hear that we can do whatever we want with
our bodies—use them for pleasure and gratifica-
tion, destroy them through alcohol or drugs or
over-exercising, even use others' bodies for our
own pleasure. All of this is a very real temptation,
especially for a teen in today's society. It's hard with
all the messages coming through the media and
through peer pressure to remember that my body
is a temple of the Holy Spirit. And this presence of
the Holy Spirit makes my body holy. It's pretty wild
to think about—my body is holy! The challenge
that this verse offers me is to constantly remember
that the presence of God in me is making my body

holy, and then to treat myself in that way. While the media tell me not to be happy unless my body is "perfect," this verse tells me I can be happy and respect my body exactly as it is, because God lives within me.

*∼ Steve*

## Don't risk the danger of turning away from God

" . . . *do not make room for the devil*" (Ephesians 4:27).

This verse means a lot to me because it tells me that my actions should never put me in danger of turning away from God. You should never do something that will put you at risk of sinning and pushing away from God, leaving room for the devil to come into your life. If that happens, it takes courage and faith to push the devil away and bring God back into your life.

∼ *Mara*

## Obstacles can strengthen us

*"Woe to the world because of things that cause sin! Such things must come, but woe to the one through whom they come!" (Matthew 18:7 NAB).*

Sometimes when I am put in a difficult situation, I wonder why God has let it happen. From this Scripture passage I realized that God allows these obstacles for a reason—to strengthen me and help me learn how to overcome temptation. This verse also tells me to stay away from the people who bring temptation into my life.

*∼ Maria*

## How to find true happiness

*"Child, remember that during your lifetime you received your good things, and Lazarus in like manner evil things; but now he is comforted here, and you are in agony" (Luke 16:25).*

This passage reminds me of the lesson Jesus taught about how in heaven the last shall be first and the first shall be last. It is all about how much we nurture heavenly and spiritual things and not worldly or material things. It is easy to fall for all the materialism of this world. We are bombarded from all angles by TV ads, magazines, stores, and even other people, to buy more, get more, accumulate more. We want the latest things, the coolest gadgets, and it is never enough because new things keep coming out. However, when we concentrate on wealth and material things, there is no room for God in our lives. The life of a Christian is a life that thinks of others first, serves God, and rejects evil. If we forget God now, will he open the door of heaven to us at the last minute when we are asking to be let in, just like the unprepared maids awaiting the bridegroom? They did not prepare themselves, they were foolish, and when the time came, they missed it all. I do not want to be caught up in the search for happiness in material things. I want to seek heavenly treasures and bring the love of Jesus to everyone I come across.

Jesus, make my heart strong and pure for you. Let me always reject the idea that wealth and things make me happy. Instead, put joy in my heart for loving you and others, and for knowing that one day, you and I will be together in heaven.

~ *Gabriel*

## I compete for God's glory

*"Athletes exercise self-control in all things; they do it to receive a perishable wreath, but we an imperishable one"* (1 Corinthians 9:25).

As a high school athlete, sometimes it is easy to be caught up in being "the best." Getting your name in the paper, receiving congratulations from all your classmates, and being the center of attention after a winning game or meet can be a lot of fun. However, many athletes, even Christian ones, can become sidetracked from the true reason they compete. Looking around my school, I see that the soccer player or elite runner that began as a freshman phenomenon can quickly become an arrogant athlete that no one looks up to. It is a twisting trap. The glories of winning are very appealing, but so are many things that we should turn away from. Instead, we are called to give the glory to our Lord. This is still possible even while maintaining a highly competitive spirit. Thanking

God for giving you the strength, health, talent, and love for a game can be just as rewarding as hearing the roar of the cheering stands. When you step onto the field, never forget who guides your steps and presents you with the opportunities to glorify him.

Heavenly Father, as I compete to the best of my ability, guide my steps and those of my teammates. Help me strive to glorify you with my actions, through victory and defeat. Amen.

∼ *Colleen*

# FORGIVENESS

# A PRAYER FOR FORGIVENESS

Have mercy on me, O God,
>according to your steadfast love;
according to your abundant mercy
>blot out my transgressions.
Wash me thoroughly from my iniquity,
>and cleanse me from my sin.
For I know my transgressions,
>and my sin is ever before me.
Against you, you alone, have I sinned,
>and done what is evil in your sight,
so that you are justified in your sentence. . . .
Create in me a clean heart, O God,
>and put a new and right spirit within me.
Do not cast me away from your presence,
>and do not take your holy spirit from me.
Restore to me the joy of your salvation,
>and sustain in me a willing spirit.

*Psalm 51:1–4, 10–11*

# Come and be forgiven

*"When Jesus saw their faith, he said to the paralytic, 'Son, your sins are forgiven'"* (Mark 2:5).

It takes great faith for our sins to be forgiven. We must also be willing. Jesus is always there to forgive sins. I just need courage to approach Jesus through the sacrament of Reconciliation. The way Jesus calls this man his "son" shows how much he cares for us. To me, we are like this paralytic man. We might not be paralyzed physically, but we might be spiritually. I think the guilt of my sin paralyzes me, but I feel relieved when I am forgiven. I truly am blessed to be healed by Jesus.

∽ *Alexandra*

## Live with a forgiving heart

*"Let anyone among you who is without sin be the first to throw a stone at her" (John 8:7).*

This Scripture verse reminds me that I am a sinner. It makes me stop trying to see how I'm better than someone else. In a home with lots of brothers and sisters, it is easy for me to be judgmental. Recalling this verse often helps me not to "throw a stone" at my siblings, whom I should love the most of all my friends. When someone wears my sneakers to take the dog out, and they end up soaking wet, I should just forgive and forget the incident rather than creating an argument. Maybe they couldn't find their shoes because the baby took them and put them behind the couch.

The challenge this Scripture verse gives us is that we should be more forgiving, like Jesus in this story, because we want people to forgive us when we offend them. I definitely don't want a stone thrown at me, so why would I pick up a stone to throw at someone else?

~ *Teresa*

## God will always welcome us back

*"Why do you raise such questions in your hearts?"* *(Mark 2:8).*

There are many times when we question Jesus and his miracles. I know there have been times when I have questioned my faith in Jesus. It wasn't until my darkest moments and my worst experiences that I realized that Jesus is really there for me always. I realized that our God is a merciful, forgiving God and that he loves us no matter what we do. It doesn't matter how much we doubt and question him, when we want to come back to him he's always there with open arms welcoming us back.

~ *Kimberly*

## Forgiveness brings peace

*"For if you forgive others their trespasses, your heavenly Father will also forgive you"* (Matthew 6:14).

This passage particularly jumps out at me as being one of the most important messages that God communicates to his people. Forgiveness is one of the most essential virtues that humans can have. God calls us to turn the other cheek. Throughout my life, I have learned that it is much better to forgive than to hold a grudge. By learning to forgive others, I have grown as a person and I live a more positive life. By focusing on the flaws of others, we draw ourselves away from God's love and mercy, but when we forgive others, we are blessed with God's love and receive his forgiveness.

*∼ Edward*

## Put your hope for forgiveness in God

*"For you, O LORD, are my hope, my trust, O LORD, from my youth" (Psalm 71:5).*

These words have had a great impact on me because of how true they are. God is my hope. He is the one I pray to when I need help, when I need forgiveness for something I have done wrong, and even when I am scared or sad. He is always there when I really need him and he always will be; he is my confidence.

≈ *Chloe*

# God gives us a new beginning

*"Then he came forward and touched the bier, and the bearers stood still. And he said, 'Young man, I say to you, rise!'" (Luke 7:14).*

The raising of the widow's son is a powerful demonstration of the love which changes everything. Our life can never be the same again when the powerful love of God breaks into our life and makes it new. Through his powerful love for us, he gives us a new beginning and we set out on a journey that leads to the glory of God's presence. This miracle helps me think about the wonderful miracle of Jesus' resurrection from the dead. In the great miracle of rising from the dead, we have the promise of our resurrection when we are raised to eternal life. He speaks his word to me to give renewed hope, strength, and courage to follow him in all things, and to serve others with a glad and generous heart.

~ *Alejandra*

# I am always God's child

*"Son, you are always with me, and all that is mine is yours. But we had to celebrate and rejoice, because this brother of yours was . . . lost and has been found"* (Luke 15:31–32).

The last two sentences of the story of the Prodigal Son are near and dear to me. These few words of Jesus have a significant impact on how I live. These words affirm that we will always be children of God and share in his love and divinity. More importantly, however, the parable serves as evidence that God is forgiving to those who have strayed from him and have found their way back. His words here provide me with that inner solace, that no matter how badly or how often I may have turned my back on him, God will always welcome me back with open arms and continue to love me as he does all his children. God's almost unbelievable capacity for forgiveness, as portrayed in these lines, gives me inspiration and carries me through each new day in my life.

~ *Christopher*

## Leave the judging to God

*"Why do you see the speck in your neighbor's eye, but do not notice the log in your own eye?" (Luke 6:41).*

God teaches us about judging others in this quote. We find it easier to look at and judge our neighbors for their mistakes than to actually make our own examination of conscience and look at our faults and how we should fix them. God knows our mistakes, even when we can't seem to recognize them. That's why he is the only one who can judge all people. But just like a true father, the Lord forgives and leads us away from sin. Reading this quote, I realize that God is leading me away from hypocrisy by helping me to notice and admit to my own wrongdoing instead of that of my neighbors. I pray to God to help me get closer to him instead of criticizing others; that way, I will look at the good in the people around me.

∼ *Andres*

# VIRTUE

# A PRAYER TO LEAD A VIRTUOUS LIFE

Hear, O Israel: The LORD is our God, the LORD
    alone.
You shall love the LORD your God with all your
    heart,
and with all your soul, and with all your might.
Keep these words that I am commanding you
    today in your heart.
Recite them to your children and talk about them
when you are at home and when you are away,
when you lie down and when you rise.
Bind them as a sign on your hand,
fix them as an emblem on your forehead,
and write them on the doorposts of your house
    and on your gates.

*Deuteronomy 6:4–9*

# The Golden Rule

*"In everything do to others as you would have them do to you; for this is the law and the prophets" (Matthew 7:12).*

I have always seen this quote as playing a key role in my life. I have heard it in another way, but it means the same: "Do unto others as you would want them to do unto you." No matter how people treat me or what they say to me, I should always treat them the way I would want to be treated. I think this is something that everyone should follow. If everyone would treat others the way that they want to be treated, the world would be a better, more peaceful place. I know that it is important to treat others with respect, even though sometimes it can be difficult. But I always try my hardest to treat others with respect. I will often ask God to give me the strength and wisdom to do what he wants me to do.

$\sim$ *Melissa*

## Love your enemies

*"Love your enemies and pray for those who persecute you"* *(Matthew 5:44).*

This is perhaps the greatest challenge Jesus puts before us. Most people, and I include myself, feel that our "enemies" do not deserve to be treated with love or kindness because they should get a "taste of their own medicine." However, loving our enemies, which could be those who hate us, insult us, or are intolerant and critical of us, can only be accomplished with God's grace. When we pray for our persecutors, we also receive a special grace from God to love and act with mercy toward them. Prayer has the power to transform their hearts as well as ours. I pray that I may be showered with the special grace from the Lord to love those who hurt me and that I may act as Jesus wants me to. I ask the Lord to let me be like him in compassion and mercy.

$\sim$ *Gabriel*

# Witness for Christ

*"But you will receive power when the Holy Spirit has come upon you; and you will be my witnesses . . . to the ends of the earth" (Acts 1:8).*

It's hard to explain the impact that these words have had on my life. This was the theme for a diocesan youth event that I attended. I had never thought that *I* could be a witness for Christ, that I could speak to others about him. But to hear this Scripture say that I would receive the power to do that? That just blew my mind. I felt and still feel that all of us teens (all Christians, actually) have been sent by the Holy Spirit to make a difference in the world. There are so many people I see every day who don't have any idea of what their life could be like. They need Christ. I want to be his witness to them.

~ *Patrick*

## Focus on the important things in life

*"Do not store up for yourselves treasures on earth, where moth and rust consume and where thieves break in and steal; but store up for yourselves treasures in heaven, where neither moth nor rust consumes and where thieves do not break in and steal"* (Matthew 6:19–20).

I think this is a very important message that Jesus gives us. Often we get so caught up in our worldly possessions or money that we lose focus on other more important things in our lives. I sometimes find myself becoming obsessed with things that I later realize are actually unimportant. Right here in this passage, Jesus is telling us that we shouldn't be so worried about investing in earthly possessions because in the end, they are worthless. He's telling us that instead of investing our time and money in these unimportant things, we should invest in the treasures of heaven. We should invest our time in things like building a stronger relationship with God, and we should invest our extra money in giving to those who have nothing. I think that this verse is especially important today because today's society is all about money and the cool things that you have. I believe this one Scripture quote could be sort of a wakeup call to people everywhere, like it was for me.

∽ *Kimberly*

## Accept others' differences

*"Jesus stretched out his hand and touched [the man with leprosy], and said to him, 'I do choose. Be made clean!'"* (Mark 1:41).

Jesus didn't care that this man had an infectious disease; he was compassionate toward the man, *touched* him, and healed him.

You may think that this doesn't apply to you, that you treat the sick with kindness; but almost everyone participates in some sort of prejudice. Let's replace the word "leprosy" with something else. Have you ever looked down upon someone with a disease, a different skin color, another religion, a lower intelligence, someone poor? Chances are that you have done one of these things at some point in your life. The passage isn't speaking of *just* leprosy. It is more of a symbol of all the things that can cause someone to be looked down upon.

This passage helped me realize how sometimes I look down upon someone just because they are different. I worry so much about how people would look at me if I treated that person with kindness that I begin to forget that God is the only one I need to please. When I die, God isn't going to judge me on my popularity. He is going to see how pure my heart and soul are. I am going to try to be nicer to people who are different from now on.

*∼ Erica*

## Jesus' love changes us

*"I give you a new commandment, that you love one another. Just as I have loved you, you also should love one another" (John 13:34).*

This new commandment given to us from Jesus has really helped me to change the way I live. I used to go to lunch and gossip about people the whole time. Then, I started to try and love others as Jesus loves me. Jesus loved me enough to die for me, so I know that he would never go behind my back and gossip, because that would hurt me. Realizing that gossiping hurts others, I stopped. If you truly love someone, you do not want to hurt them.

Before trying to live this new commandment, I was very hesitant about evangelizing at my public school. My thoughts were that I didn't need to go telling everyone about Jesus, and how we can be saved by following him. But if you love someone, shouldn't you help to save them? I realized that when you love someone, you try to do what is the best for them. You want them to be protected from harm and be in eternal happiness. I now try my hardest not to gossip, and take every chance I can to tell others about Christ.

*~ Lannah*

## Faith is believing without seeing

*"[Jesus] said to Thomas, 'Put your finger here and see my hands. Reach out your hand and put it in my side. Do not doubt but believe.' Thomas answered him, 'My Lord and my God!' Jesus said to him, 'Have you believed because you have seen me? Blessed are those who have not seen and yet have come to believe'"* (John 20:27–29).

The story of doubting Thomas has always been one of my favorite Bible passages, but as a teen growing in faith it has taken on significant meaning. This story draws a strong parallel not only to me individually, but also to our society. In a world dominated by fact and proof, we often lose focus on what aspect of our life is most important: faith. I believe even the most faithful followers of our religion struggle, and can fall victim to doubt just as Thomas did. Yet Jesus lives within us and works through us; why do we need to see to believe? We do not. We must strive to be the "blessed" disciple and believe without seeing.

*∾ Daniel*

## Have a big heart

*"If you love those who love you, what credit is that to you?" (Luke 6:32).*

This quote struck me because it shows what high standards God has for us. In today's society, we never take certain sins as a big deal. We often take things too lightly when they are really very serious. It does not take much to love someone who treats you well. You are not making a difference in the world that way. God is saying it takes a lot to love someone who treats us badly or ignores us, and that doing so makes a huge difference. Also, when you love someone who hates you, you don't have to live with the feelings of vengeance and holding grudges. So, in a way, it is like a reward here in this life and an even greater one in heaven.

~ *Heather*

# PRAYER

# A PRAYER TO PRAISE GOD

Praise the LORD!
Praise God in his sanctuary;
    praise him in his mighty firmament!
Praise him for his mighty deeds;
    praise him according to his surpassing
    greatness!
Praise him with trumpet sound;
    praise him with lute and harp!
Praise him with tambourine and dance;
    praise him with strings and pipe!
Praise him with clanging cymbals;
    praise him with loud clashing cymbals!
Let everything that breathes praise the LORD!
Praise the LORD!

*Psalm 150*

# Pay attention—Jesus is here!

*"For where two or three are gathered in my name, I am there among them" (Matthew 18:20).*

That's a pretty big promise. I witnessed this last year on my drive to school. My older brother drove us every morning and afternoon. When you live 45 minutes from school, that's a lot of time in the car. Every day, however, I felt God join us on our commute. He spoke in our conversations and sat with us in our silences. He was with us in those 45-minute drives, and he used every second.

Now I look at every minute spent with followers of Christ as a chance to invite Jesus to join us, even if it seems like dead time when nothing is really going on. No matter where we are, or what we're doing, Jesus will join us, and make that moment a billion times better.

⁓ *Olivia*

## God waits for us in prayer

*"He came out and went, as was his custom, to the Mount of Olives; and the disciples followed him. When he reached the place, he said to them, 'Pray that you may not come into the time of trial.' Then he withdrew from them about a stone's throw, knelt down, and prayed" (Luke 22:39–41).*

There's a certain solemnity, a certain depth that is present in this passage. In my Spanish language Bible, the words are more closely translated to, "Pray that you may not fall into temptation." Seeing what Jesus did so close to his time of suffering and death is a beautiful reminder to remain praying *with* Christ, as he invited his disciples to. We should pray that we may not fall into temptation: the temptation of contempt toward another person, the temptation of feeling incompetent, the temptation of fear, the temptation to despair.

In my own life, through hardships such as my parents' separation, and with the scattered memories of the country I left as a young child and the complete uncertainty about the future and college, I often find myself tempted to despair and to extract only bitterness from the silence around me. This passage reminds me of the love that is found in prayer. It is necessary to return to prayer even amid chaos, trusting that in solitude, on that Mount of Olives, God is waiting for us, ready to give us hope and fortitude.

~ *Sofía*

# God is my friend—through good times and bad

*"Ask, and it will be given you; search, and you will find; knock, and the door will be opened for you. For everyone who asks receives, and everyone who searches finds, and for everyone who knocks, the door will be opened" (Matthew 7:7–8).*

I've heard many inspiring stories of God coming into people's lives and working miracles. Although I am blessed with many things, I've also had my share of misfortune. During difficult times, I've felt abandoned. This causes me to resent God for helping others in their time of need and neglecting me. I avoid posing this very important question: "Did I seek God?" The answer, of course, is no. I am usually too busy thinking of the obstacles in my life to stop and ask God for his help. It's wrong to expect him just to come and help whenever I need him, while I've completely ignored him through good times and bad. A very wise teacher once told me, "You can't treat God like some sort of gumball machine, dispensing candy whenever you need it." God is more like a friend. If one of your closest friends had become distant from you, but then suddenly came to you because they wanted something from you, wouldn't you be offended? You would, because a relationship in which a person is used only for personal gain is completely wrong. We need to seek God, during good times and bad. It's time we stopped expecting him to magically appear when things go wrong, and started seeking his love through prayer and the sacraments.

~ *Lisa*

## Be still and listen

*"[Jesus] entered a certain village, where a woman named Martha welcomed him into her home. She had a sister named Mary, who sat at the Lord's feet and listened to what he was saying. But Martha was distracted by her many tasks; so she came to him and asked, 'Lord, do you not care that my sister has left me to do all the work by myself? Tell her then to help me.' But the Lord answered her, 'Martha, Martha, you are worried and distracted by many things; there is need of only one thing. Mary has chosen the better part, which will not be taken away from her'"* (Luke 10:38–42).

When I think of this Scripture verse, I often think of myself as Martha. School, chores, and all the other activities I am involved in seem to take up so much time, and leave me very few moments with God. I like to keep busy and do many things, but sometimes I find myself doing too much and worrying instead of thinking of God. It is a real challenge for me to sit still in the midst of a busy life, like Mary did, and listen to God.

My family goes to daily Mass, and as I sit in the pew looking at the tabernacle, I feel God's presence so very close to me. I realize that I have the chance every day to be more like Mary, as I am so near to Jesus in the Eucharist. I picture myself sitting at Jesus' feet, and I feel a special sense of peace in my heart. After Mass is over, I leave all my worries behind at the feet of Jesus, and I try to become more like Mary, who chose the better part.

*∼ Mary Clare*

## Praise God no matter what

*"I will bless the LORD at all times; his praise continually be in my mouth" (Psalm 34:1).*

I referred to this Scripture for over a year's time when I was praying to reunite a brother and sister because they desperately needed each other. These two little children who had been separated had very little chance of being together. I prayed to God every day, and I told him that even though I was afraid, I would never give up hope, and that I would always love him and praise him at all times, no matter what happened. Then, through constant prayer and constant praise, the most amazing thing happened. Through that praise, God granted the blessing of these two children being reunited as my new adopted brother and sister. Every time I am having a hard time in my life, this Scripture passage helps me to get through it. It reminds me of the miracle God gave me to experience, and it reminds me to praise him no matter what comes along.

∼ *Sarah*

## Pray with awareness

*"Could you not keep awake one hour?" (Mark 14:37).*

Like Peter in the garden, sometimes I feel like I'm sleeping in my faith, or more accurately, I'm sleepwalking. I say prayers and I believe in God, but I don't really think about why I'm praying or why I believe. With this passage, Jesus is calling me to stay awake with him always.

∼ *Meg*

# Come to Jesus with an open heart

*"Whoever becomes humble like this child is the greatest in the kingdom of heaven. Whoever welcomes one such child in my name welcomes me" (Matthew 18:4–5).*

Jesus is very humble and always comes to us in a humble manner, so this is how he wants us to approach him. He only wishes for us to come to him with an open heart. We can tell Jesus anything we want and speak to him about anything that is troubling us. Jesus always receives us with open arms and turns away no one. In the ancient world children had little or no worth. They were looked down upon. Jesus will never look down on us. We are his children, and he loves us just as our fathers and mothers love us, and even more. When Jesus took the children up into his arms in the Scripture passage, he wanted to show his disciples that children were very humble and that this is the same way we should come to Jesus.

~ *Cristina*

## Jesus prays with us

*"Now during those days he went out to the mountain to pray; and he spent the night in prayer to God" (Luke 6:12).*

I love this verse because so often I forget that Jesus prayed, too. And he still prays to the Father in the unity of the Trinity. We must always have our hearts offered up to God and strive to live in union with him. That way we will be praying with Jesus to the Father, and his will shall be done.

~ *Laura*

# DAILY LIFE

# A PRAYER FOR DAILY LIVING

Love is patient; love is kind;
love is not envious or boastful or arrogant
    or rude.
It does not insist on its own way;
it is not irritable or resentful;
it does not rejoice in wrongdoing,
but rejoices in the truth.
It bears all things, believes all things,
hopes all things, endures all things.
Love never ends.

*1 Corinthians 13:4–8*

## God is bigger

*"We know that all things work together for good for those who love God, who are called according to his purpose" (Romans 8:28).*

My life as a teenager goes up and down. I struggle with "fitting in," keeping my grades up, and balancing a hectic lifestyle. With every minute of the day packed, when something goes wrong, it is easy to get stressed and freak out. Knowing that Jesus has a reason for everything has truly changed my life.

I switched schools this year (junior year) to a much more academically challenging school. My grades dropped drastically, and I don't really fit in at the school. Because of this Bible verse, I am able to realize that God is with me through everything and that he is bigger than me. When I turn my life over to him, everything is a grace!

∼ *Lylah*

## God wants the best for me

*"For surely I know the plans I have for you, says the LORD, plans for your welfare and not for harm, to give you a future with hope"* (Jeremiah 29:11).

This verse from Jeremiah shines with a brilliance of comfort and joy. It has long been the idea that gets me through uncertain times, like when I question how a difficult situation could possibly turn out well, or whether I will choose the right college, career, or vocation. In those times, I turn to this verse as a basis for trust in God and belief that he is both an almighty God who is greater than any of my struggles, and a caring and loving Father who is personally interested in my life and actually *wants the best for me* just as much as I do, if not more so. God is good, God loves me, and God knows what he's doing.

~ Catherine

# God gives me all that I have

*"Look at the birds of the air; they neither sow nor reap nor gather into barns, and yet your heavenly Father feeds them. Are you not of more value than they?"* (Matthew 6:26).

I like this quote just because of its simplicity. It tells me not to worry because everything is in God's hands. God knows my needs, and so far in my life he has given me all that I have. I have the ability to go to a Catholic school. I am healthy and have been blessed with an amazing family. I also have very good friends who know practically everything about me. I thank God every day for all of my blessings. Even though I have been through some rough times, God, who is 100 percent reliable, has helped me through them. I trust in God who knows me better than anybody and has truly blessed me.

∼ *Victoria*

## Nervous? Talk to God

*"Cast all your anxiety on him, because he cares for you" (1 Peter 5:7).*

This Bible verse affects me in many ways. But the most important way it has affected me has to do with my color guard competitions. I started color guard this year and it was my first time doing such a thing. I love it, but it was my first competition experience, and I was really nervous that I would mess up when I got up to perform in front of so many people. Before the music started I said a little prayer. All I really said was, "God, please help me and the rest of the team do everything right, help us forget that there are people watching us, help us go out there and perform our hearts out and maybe place, and help me feel the music instead of losing myself in the counts." I turned it all over to God. The music started and before I knew it, it was my part. I performed perfectly. I was amazed at how well I did, how the audience seemed to disappear when I got out there, how I forgot the counts and just used my memory. When it was time to find out our places, I was surprised when they announced that our team won first place in our division. I know God always cares about us and takes away our worries. He listened to me that night!

∽ *Elizabeth*

## Jesus is strength for every weakness

*" . . . for whenever I am weak, then I am strong"*
*(2 Corinthians 12:10).*

When I listen to these words from Saint Paul, I think of the difficulties of high school. I think of my long commute, the difficult courses, or being made fun of by some students because I was a campus minister. I recall what it was like not to be able to hear most of the lectures due to auditory processing delays and how hard it was to sit through them with attention deficit disorder. Now, I am almost ready to graduate, and I am at the end of the race. As I look back, I realize that I have been made stronger through my weaknesses. As Christians, we are called to identify with Jesus in his passion. When we are given crosses, we must pick them up and carry them. These crosses will bring us closer to God and make us better people.

∽ *Matthew*

## Choosing friends

*"If your hand causes you to sin, cut it off. It is better for you to enter into life maimed than with two hands to go . . . into the unquenchable fire"* (Mark 9:43 *NAB*).

Once I had a best friend whom I always spent time with in middle school. In the summer before high school, he began acting up and doing drugs. He was becoming farther away from God, and he was taking me with him. I had to end the relationship because he was trying to make me give up my faith. In the end it was a good decision, because I see him now and I realize that I didn't need him and that I'm better off without him.

*~ Michael*

## Compassion makes a difference

*"He stretched out his hand and touched him, saying, 'I do choose. Be made clean!' Immediately his leprosy was cleansed"* (Matthew 8:3).

By curing this man of leprosy, Jesus made his life a lot better. This man was an outcast, shunned because of his disease. The way Jesus showed compassion and mercy toward him is something many of us nowadays do not even try to do. Many people around us are considered outcasts or rejects, and having a friend can make all the difference for them. For instance, if there is someone in school who is alone a lot of the time and appears not to have many friends, it would be right for us to go and talk to him or her and be friendly. That can completely change the person's life for the better. I am a friendly person, and I enjoy befriending people who are alone because not only do I feel good for what I did, I make a new friend in the process.

$\sim$ *Monica*

# Living my faith as a teen today

*"Let no one despise your youth, but set the believers an example in speech and conduct, in love, in faith, in purity" (1 Timothy 4:12).*

Set an example. These words that God commanded us to do are big. Trying to live out the faith as a teen in today's world is not easy, but God still tells us that we are the ones who should be setting an example. At those times when I feel like nothing I do will make a difference, thinking back to this passage gives me courage. My actions do matter. It reminds me to keep God in my heart at all times, and to reflect his love through everything I do. It is a big task, and I know that when I fail, he is still there to pick me up and help me try again.

∼ *Julie*

## Work with all your heart

*"Whatever you do, do from the heart, as for the Lord and not for others" (Colossians 3:23 NAB).*

This passage has been a guiding force in my life ever since I was introduced to it in seventh grade. Here, God's word holds a dual meaning. The first meaning of this passage is that God calls us to work at everything as hard as we can. God wants us to work with *all* of our heart as if we are working for him. In my life, it has meant trying to devote myself 100 percent to whatever I do, from my studies to serving my community. I know I would be giving every ounce of effort I had if I were working for the Lord, and that's how I try to approach every task in my life. The second meaning of this passage calls us to work with our *heart*, with compassion in our lives. As Christians, we must try to emulate Jesus, which means incorporating compassion into everything we do in life. In all of our work, we must never forget the importance of charity and using both our brain and our heart. Incorporating the two meanings of this passage has helped guide me through the toughest decisions of my life.

∽ *Hunter*

# Do your best and rely on God

*"What deeds of power are being done by his hands!"*
*(Mark 6:2).*

God, the creator of all good, power, and love, is mindful of me. Why should I be afraid when all power rests in the loving arms of my Father? What is there to worry about when I do not control anything, but all that I do comes from God? What evil malice can afflict me if I am held safely in God's all-powerful love? This passage really speaks to me in my everyday life. Between school work, family, colleges, friends, and extracurricular activities, I do not have a lot of time. In the midst of all the noise, I hear God tell me, "Why rush? Take one minute and talk to me." My response is, "I would love to, except I have so many different things, which you have inspired me to do." But then I realize that if God is inspiring all that I do, why can I not take some quiet time to talk to him? After all, if he instructed me to accomplish so many tasks, then he will finish what he began. It is not I working alone who will be accepted into college, or I who will receive an "A" on a test by myself, but God will work through me to accomplish these things. This does not mean we should not use our talents to the best of our abilities; it just means that while we work so hard, we cannot forget to rely on and talk to our all-powerful God.

*∼ Kathryn*

## Keep the focus of your heart on God

*"You cannot serve God and wealth. Therefore I tell you, do not worry about your life, what you will eat or what you will drink, or about your body, what you will wear. Is not life more than food, and the body more than clothing?"* (Matthew 6:24–25).

I like this verse because it really reflects how society is, even today. By "wealth," Jesus meant money or any materialistic possessions. It's impossible to focus on God when we're too busy thinking of our possessions or what we look like. The media are always putting people down for how they look or what type of lifestyle they have. And because of that, people begin obsessing over things which pull them away and separate them from God. Of course, our appearance can sometimes be important, but we shouldn't take it to an extreme level. Instead, all of us should care about better things in life, like serving God and living up to his expectations. Jesus tells all of us to put away all the preoccupation with those materialistic things and instead find the things of God, which are his kingdom and righteousness. So, I ask Jesus to take me away from these pointless worries, and to help me live my life making God my main focus.

~ *Andres*

# OTHER
# HELPFUL STUFF

# HOW TO LOOK UP A PASSAGE IN THE BIBLE

Here's the key to crack the code of Scripture citations.

You may see something like this: Jn 3:16.

The first part refers to the "book" of the Bible. The Bible is really a collection of seventy-three short books. Sometimes in a citation the name of the book is written out (John), but often it is abbreviated (Jn). In the front of your Bible, you can find a list of the books and their abbreviations.

The next part, the first number ("3"), refers to the chapter of the book.

The part after the colon ("16") refers to the verse of the chapter. In some Bibles, the verse numbers are written in the text itself; in others, the verse numbers run alongside the text, in the margin. (Sometimes the citation has a comma instead of a colon, like this: Jn 3, 16.)

So, the citation above is from the Gospel according to John. Go to chapter 3 and find verse 16. "For God so loved the world that he gave his only Son, so that everyone who believes in him may not perish but may have eternal life."

# HOW TO PRAY WITH SCRIPTURE (LECTIO DIVINA)

### How can I pray with Scripture?

The young people who contributed to this book have shared what they have heard God saying to them through Scripture. There are many ways of opening ourselves to God's Word. One way of praying with Scripture that has been practiced since the early days of Christianity is *Lectio Divina* (pronounced "LEX-ee-o di-VEE-nah"), which literally means "holy reading."

### How can I pray Lectio Divina?

*Lectio Divina* has six main steps:

    1. Pray to the Holy Spirit.

2. *Lectio:* read the Scripture text.

3. *Meditatio* ("med-i-TAH-tsee-o"): meditate or reflect on the text.

4. *Oratio* ("o-RAH-tsee-o"): pray with the text.

5. *Contemplatio* ("con-tem-PLAH-tsee-o"): contemplate or rest in God's Word.

6. Pray in thanksgiving.

The first step is to *pray to the Holy Spirit.* You might use one of the prayers in the back of this book, another prayer that you know, or your own words to ask the Holy Spirit to be with you and help you understand God's Word.

The next step is to *read the text.* Here's an example from the Gospel of Matthew so you can try it out:

Now the eleven disciples went to Galilee, to the mountain to which Jesus had directed them. When they saw him, they worshiped him; but some doubted. And Jesus came and said to them, "All authority in heaven and on earth has been given to me. Go therefore and make disciples of all nations, baptizing them in the name of the Father and of the Son and of the Holy Spirit, and teaching them to obey everything that I have commanded you. And remember, I am with you always, to the end of the age." (Matthew 28:16–20)

Read it slowly, once or twice, maybe even aloud. Ask yourself, what is happening in the text? In this passage, we see the disciples going to *meet* Jesus and worshiping him, but at the same time doubting him. Jesus *approaches* and comes close to them. Then he *speaks* to them and gives them his own power. Finally, he *promises* to be with them always. We can ask ourselves questions, such as: what were the disciples feeling? How did Jesus look and sound? This was the last time the disciples would see him on earth. What did he want to share with them? Also, notice whether a particular word or phrase speaks to you; for instance, "Jesus approached" or "I am with you always."

*Next, reflect. Go a little bit deeper.* Ask yourself not just what the text is saying, but what is it saying to *me*? What does God desire to tell me? How is he inviting me to grow or change? For example, as I notice how Jesus approaches the disciples, I may consider how Jesus approaches and comes close to me in my life. I might reflect on Jesus' desire to draw close to me, and on how I recognize his presence in my life. I can ask myself why Jesus approaches me: to give me his love and his grace, and to send me out as he sent the disciples. I might also reflect on the areas of my life that I keep closed to Jesus and how I can open them to his love.

*The next step is to pray.* God has offered me an invitation—how will I respond? In this passage, Jesus has invited me to be more aware of how he approaches and comes close to me. I can pray for the grace to recognize his presence throughout the day. I can tell Jesus that his invitation makes me feel excited, but a little frightened at the same time. During this time, really enter into conversation with God. He speaks to you through his Word, and he wants to hear what you have to say!

Then, *rest in the Word that God has spoken to you.* It can help to think of a short prayer or a phrase from the Scripture passage to accompany you throughout your day. For example, I might keep in my mind the words, "Jesus approached," or I might turn these words into a prayer: "Jesus, come close to me today!"

Finally, as you end your *Lectio Divina,* pray in thanksgiving for God's word and ask him for the grace and strength to live his invitation to you.

### Can I pray Lectio Divina in a group?

When prayed in a group, *Lectio Divina* follows a similar pattern. First, pray to the Holy Spirit. Then, have one or two people *read the Scripture passage aloud.* Share with one another what you notice: the people, the places, the actions, and so forth.

Next, *share with one another what the text is saying to you personally.* How is God speaking to you through this passage, and how is he inviting you to grow or change?

Each person can close by *sharing a brief prayer* asking for grace and strength to respond to God's invitation. Or, each person can say a short prayer for the person next to him or her, asking God to deepen the Word in this person's life.

Finally, *close in prayer together.* This could take the form of having each person pray aloud a word or phrase from the passage that touched him or her, or it could be as simple as praying the Our Father. The richness of God's Word unfolds abundantly when we share it with one another.

### What Scripture passages should I use to pray Lectio Divina?

Any Scripture passage can be used to pray *Lectio Divina.* It is often helpful to begin with the Gospels. One way to choose a Scripture passage is to use the readings from the Mass of the day. The Sunday readings rotate in a three-year cycle: Year A, Year B, and Year C. The weekday readings are arranged in a two-year cycle: Year 1 and Year 2. The Church has organized it this way to nourish us with God's Word every day. So take advantage!

Below are some Web sites that provide information on how to find the daily readings:

www.usccb.org/nab
www.universalis.com/mass
www.dailygospel.org

There are also cell phone applications, such as iMissal, that provide the readings from the liturgy for each day.

Another way to pray *Lectio Divina* is to choose one book of the Bible and read your way through it. The best way to do this is to start not at the beginning of the Bible with the book of Genesis, but with one of the Gospels: Matthew, Mark, Luke, or John. They are usually more familiar and easier to use for prayer.

God has so much to tell you! "Put out into the deep" (Lk 5:4) of his Word, and let it transform your life!

# PRAYERS TO THE HOLY SPIRIT

## Prayer before Reading Sacred Scripture

Dear Jesus,
I believe that you are with me,
that you are present in your Word,
and that you want to speak to me.
I bring myself before you now.
I ask you to teach me, enlighten me,
and fill my heart with your grace.
May your Word, spoken so long ago,
yet spoken in a new way to me today,
draw me always closer to you. Amen.

*(Based on a prayer by Blessed James Alberione)*

## Prayer after Reading Sacred Scripture

Jesus Master,
you have the words of eternal life.
I believe in your Word of love;
increase my faith.
You have invited me to follow you;
I love you with all my mind, strength, and heart.
You are Goodness Itself;
I praise you and I thank you
for the gift of Sacred Scripture.
Like Mary, I want to remember
and preserve your words in my mind,
and treasure and meditate on them in my heart.
Strengthen me and guide me. Amen.

*(Based on a prayer by Blessed James Alberione)*

# Come, Holy Spirit

Come, Holy Spirit, come!
From heaven shed your light.
Come, Father of the poor,
shine within us and comfort us.
We welcome you as the guest of our soul.
Refresh us,
be our rest in labor,
our coolness in the heat,
our solace in sadness.
Come, most blessed Light,
shine in our hearts and fill our being.
Without you, we can do nothing good.
Heal us, renew us, wash our guilt away.
When we are stubborn, make us gentle.
When our hearts are cold, make them warm.
Guide us when we go astray.
Come, with your seven gifts;

come to us who adore you,
who want to witness to you.
Give us your salvation.
Give us your joy, your joy that never ends.
Amen. Alleluia.

*(Based on Veni, Sancte Spiritus)*

## Prayer to the Holy Spirit

Come, Holy Spirit
fill the hearts of your faithful,
and enkindle in them the fire of your love.
Send forth your Spirit, and they shall be created,
and you shall renew the face of the earth.

*(From the Novena for Pentecost)*

# Invocation to the Holy Spirit

Come, Holy Spirit.
Many times my mind is ignorant and forgetful;
come and heal my mind.
Often my will is stubborn and weak;
come and heal my will.
Many times my heart is indifferent
and not concerned for others;
come and heal my heart.
With your presence, make my mind
　　like the mind of Jesus,
make my will like the will of Jesus,
make my heart like the heart of Jesus.
Give me a new love for whatever Jesus loves
and for Jesus himself. Amen.

*(Based on a prayer by Blessed James Alberione)*

# ACKNOWLEDGMENTS

This book was created by the many teens who submitted reflections on their experience of the Word of God. It was a privilege to receive and read so many beautiful testimonies to God's grace working in the lives of young people today. We were not able to use all the materials submitted, but we extend our deepest gratitude to each person who contributed. A special thank you goes to the teachers and youth group leaders who helped us by collecting submissions from their students and youth group members:

Jean Czerniak (Children of Mary Home School, Buffalo, New York)

David Hajduk (Delbarton School, Morristown, New Jersey)

Sr. Immaculata, OCD (Archbishop Coleman
Carroll High School, Miami, Florida)

Judy Shipp (Queen of All Saints Parish,
Oakville, Missouri)

Carlyn Villani (Trinity Catholic Academy,
Brockton, Massachusetts)

. . . and all of the individual teens who shared
their reflections with us!

# CHECK THIS OUT, TOO

*Teen Prayers by Teens*

Original prayers by teens on all aspects of life. Also includes a selection of teens' favorite traditional prayers.

0-8198-7414-0
$11.95

BOOKS & MEDIA

The Daughters of St. Paul operate book and media centers at the following addresses. Visit, call, or write the one nearest you today, or find us on the World Wide Web, www.pauline.org.

**CALIFORNIA**
3908 Sepulveda Blvd, Culver City, CA 90230          310-397-8676
935 Brewster Avenue, Redwood City, CA 94063          650-369-4230
5945 Balboa Avenue, San Diego, CA 92111          858-565-9181

**FLORIDA**
145 S.W. 107th Avenue, Miami, FL 33174          305-559-6715

**HAWAII**
1143 Bishop Street, Honolulu, HI 96813          808-521-2731
Neighbor Islands call:          866-521-2731

**ILLINOIS**
172 North Michigan Avenue, Chicago, IL 60601          312-346-4228

**LOUISIANA**
4403 Veterans Memorial Blvd, Metairie, LA 70006          504-887-7631

**MASSACHUSETTS**
885 Providence Hwy, Dedham, MA 02026          781-326-5385

**MISSOURI**
9804 Watson Road, St. Louis, MO 63126          314-965-3512

**NEW YORK**
64 W. 38th Street, New York, NY 10018          212-754-1110

**PENNSYLVANIA**
Philadelphia—relocating          215-676-9494

**SOUTH CAROLINA**
243 King Street, Charleston, SC 29401          843-577-0175

**VIRGINIA**
1025 King Street, Alexandria, VA 22314          703-549-3806

**CANADA**
3022 Dufferin Street, Toronto, ON M6B 3T5          416-781-9131

¡También somos su fuente para libros,
videos y música en español!